C.E. THOMPSON

HOW DO AIRPLANES FLY?

ILLUSTRATED BY

MARCY RAMSEY

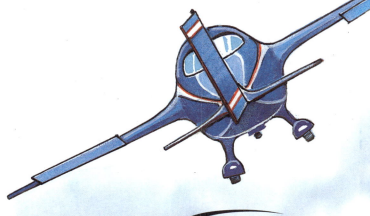

Troll

HOW DO AIRPLANES FLY?

Airplanes have engines that make them go. And they have specially shaped wings that help them fly. When air moves over the wings, it lifts up the plane.

You will understand this better when you build your airplanes and practice flying them. The instructions begin on page 28.

WHY DON'T AIRPLANES FLAP THEIR WINGS?

Airplanes can't fly the way birds do. Planes are too heavy for flapping wings to work. An airplane needs stiff wings and an engine that makes it go fast.

When a plane speeds down the runway, air moves over the wings. The wings have a special shape—curved on top and flat on the bottom.

Air moves faster across the curved top of the wing than it moves along the flat bottom. That faster-moving air helps lift the plane into the sky.

Before there were airplanes, people dreamed of flying like birds. Inventors thought machines with flapping wings would fly. But these machines were much too heavy for their wings.

Scientists who studied birds did discover something important—the curved shape of a bird's wing helps lift the bird into the air. That's why airplane wings are curved on top.

4

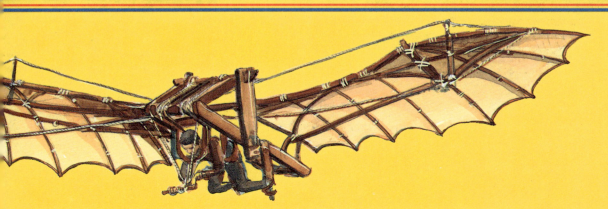

HOW DOES AIR LIFT UP AN AIRPLANE?

You can't see air, but you can feel its power when a strong wind blows. Moving air is powerful enough to lift up a heavy plane. Here's what happens:

1. The plane's engine turns the propeller. The propeller moves the plane faster and faster down the runway.

2. Wind blows over and under the wings. The air moving over the curved top of the wings has farther to go than the air moving along the bottom of the wings.

Air on the red path travels farther.

3. Because it must travel farther, the air on top of the wings must move faster and spread out. Then there is less air pressing down on top of the wings and more air pressing up under the wings.

Hold a strip of paper just below your bottom lip. Now blow out. The paper flies up. Why?

Air on the top side of the paper is moving faster than air on the bottom side of the paper. That means the air on the top side is pressing down less than the air on the bottom side.

The higher-pressure air on the bottom moves toward the lower-pressure air on top and pushes the paper up.

4. The greater air pressure under the wings pushes the wings up, and the plane takes off!

The first airplane to really fly had stiff wings and two propellers. It was built by Orville and Wilbur Wright almost a hundred years ago—about the time your great-great-grandmother was a little girl.

The kind of wings an airplane has depends on what the plane is used for.

Planes with straight wings fly well at slower speeds. An airplane that carries passengers a short distance usually has straight wings—because it doesn't need to fly superfast.

A jet plane carries passengers, mail, and other cargo for hundreds of miles (kilometers). Its swept-back wings help the jet fly faster.

An air force jet has delta wings. They are swept back for speed. And they are shaped like big triangles to help lift the plane quickly into the air.

When it came to wings, some of the first airplane designers thought more was better. Many World War I fighter planes had two or three sets of wings. Stacked wings helped the planes climb easily into the sky. But they kept these planes from going very fast.

WHAT ARE THE WINGS AT THE BACK OF THE PLANE FOR?

Those small wings are called the *stabilizer*. The stabilizer keeps the tail steady when the plane flies. Without a stabilizer the plane's tail would rock up and down. The picture shows the stabilizer and other parts of an airplane.

The *elevators* help the plane move up or down. When the elevators are down, the plane's nose points down. When the elevators are up, the plane's nose points up.

An airplane's body is called the *fuselage*.

The *rudder* helps the plane turn left or right.

Navigation lights on the wing tips help other pilots tell which way a plane is flying. The light on the left wing tip is red. The light on the right wing tip is green.

The *aileron* on each wing moves up or down to help the plane fly evenly—so it won't tip from side to side.

WHITE TAILLIGHT

RUDDER

ELEVATOR

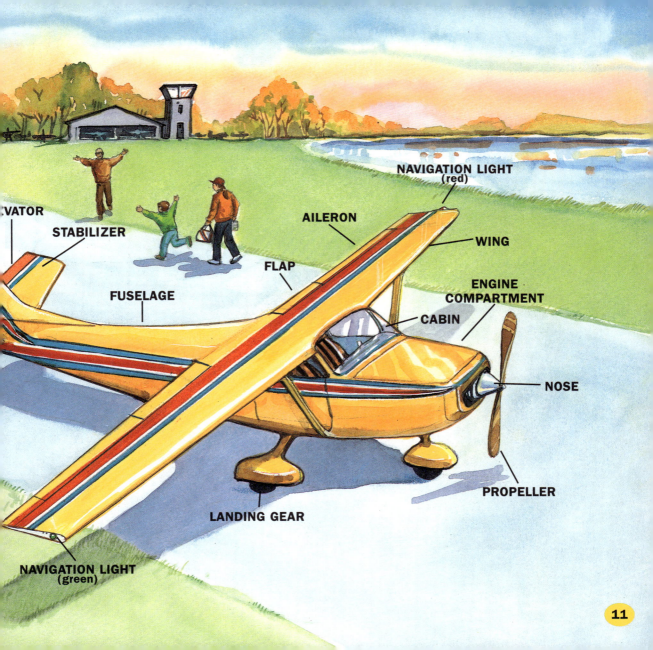

NAVIGATION LIGHT (red)

AILERON

WING

ENGINE COMPARTMENT

CABIN

NOSE

FLAP

FUSELAGE

STABILIZER

VATOR

PROPELLER

LANDING GEAR

NAVIGATION LIGHT (green)

HOW DOES AN AIRPLANE PILOT FLY THE PLANE?

The pilot moves the flight controls in the cabin, also called the flight deck, to make the plane fly. The copilot sits to the right of the pilot.

CLOCK

HORIZON INDICATOR

TACHOMETER

COMPASS

RADAR

AIRSPEED INDICATOR

ALTIMETER

FUEL GAUGE

OIL PRESSURE GAUGE

RADIO

PILOT'S SEAT

ENGINE TEMPERATURE GAUGE

ENGINE STARTING SWITCHES

YOKE

THROTTLE

RUDDER PEDAL

COPILOT'S SEAT

A plane's steering wheel is called the *yoke* or the *stick*. The *throttle* controls the speed of the engines.

The *compass* tells whether the plane is flying north, east, south, or west. The *horizon indicator* helps the pilot keep the plane level. The *airspeed indicator* shows how fast the plane is going. The *altimeter* shows how high the plane is flying.

The *radar* tells about changes in the weather and lets the pilot know if there are other planes nearby. The *radio* lets the pilot talk to traffic controllers at the airport.

WHAT MAKES THE PLANE GO UP AND DOWN?

When the pilot wants the plane to go up, he pulls back on the yoke. When he wants to take the plane down, he pushes the yoke forward.

ELEVATORS UP = TAIL DROPS

ELEVATOR

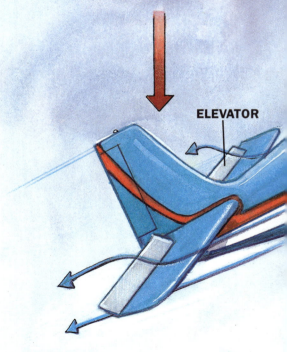

The yoke controls the elevators on the tail of the plane. When the pilot pulls back on the yoke, the elevators go up.

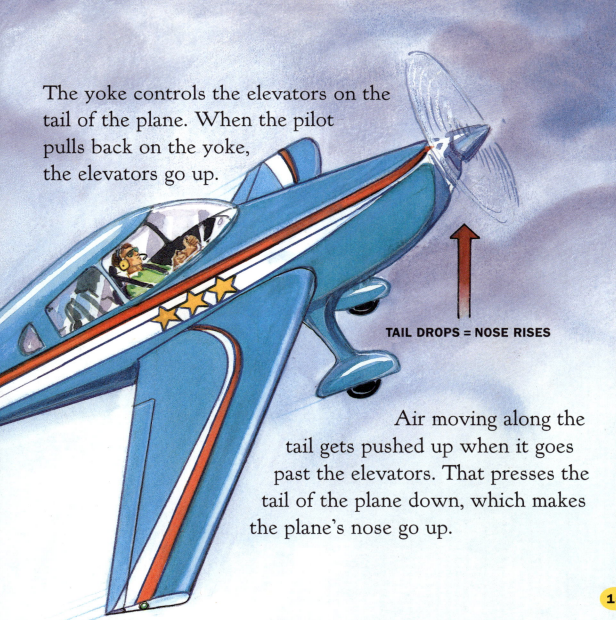

TAIL DROPS = NOSE RISES

Air moving along the tail gets pushed up when it goes past the elevators. That presses the tail of the plane down, which makes the plane's nose go up.

HOW DOES THE PILOT TURN LEFT OR RIGHT?

To make a left turn, the pilot has to do more than one thing. She pushes the left rudder pedal so that the plane's nose moves to the left. At the same time, she turns the yoke to the left. Then the plane rolls left.

When the plane turns, it goes lower in the sky. So the pilot pulls back on the yoke to make the plane fly higher. She also pushes in the throttle to make the engine go faster. It's much easier to turn left in a car than it is in a plane!

When the pilot steps on the left rudder pedal, the rudder on the plane's tail swings to the left. Air rushing past the rudder pushes the plane's nose toward the left—but that won't turn the plane completely.

The pilot must also turn the yoke left to make the aileron on the left wing go up and the aileron on the right wing go down. That gives the right wing more of a curved top than the left wing, so air moves faster over the right wing. This makes the right wing go up higher than the left wing, and the plane turns left.

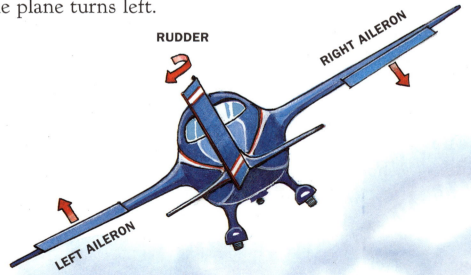

RUDDER

RIGHT AILERON

LEFT AILERON

WHAT HAPPENS WHEN A PLANE TAKES OFF?

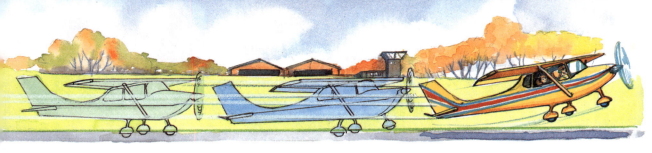

First the pilot checks all the flight controls and instruments. Then the pilot and passengers put on their seat belts. The pilot talks over the radio to the airport control tower.

The air traffic controller tells the pilot which runway to use and when to take off. The pilot hits the engine switch and pushes in the throttle. The engine roars!

The propeller begins to spin. The plane taxis onto the runway. When it's time for takeoff, the plane speeds down the runway. The pilot puts down the wing flaps. She pulls back gently on the yoke, and the plane soars up into the sky.

HOW DOES THE PILOT LAND THE PLANE?

The pilot radios an air traffic controller when the plane is near the airport. The air traffic controller tells the pilot which way to come down so her plane won't fly too close to other planes.

When the runway is clear, the pilot pulls back on the throttle to slow down the plane. She pushes the yoke in so the plane flies toward the ground. She puts down the flaps to keep the plane from coming in too fast.

The plane glides close to the ground. The pilot pulls back on the yoke to pull up the plane's nose. The landing gear bumps gently onto the runway. The pilot puts on the brakes, and the plane rolls to a stop.

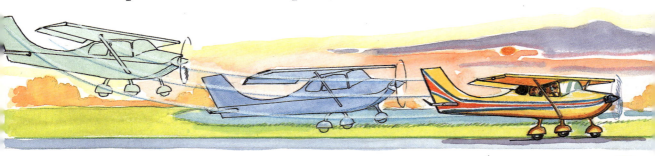

HOW MANY PEOPLE CAN AN AIRPLANE CARRY?

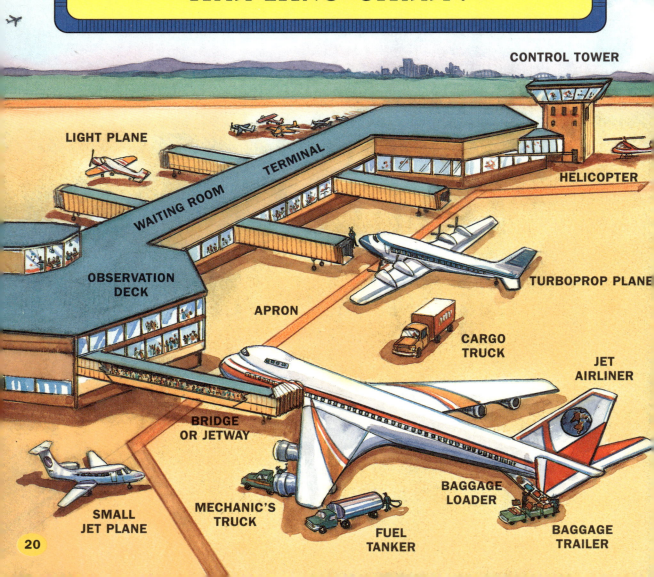

CONTROL TOWER

LIGHT PLANE

TERMINAL

WAITING ROOM

HELICOPTER

OBSERVATION DECK

APRON

TURBOPROP PLANE

CARGO TRUCK

JET AIRLINER

BRIDGE OR JETWAY

MECHANIC'S TRUCK

BAGGAGE LOADER

SMALL JET PLANE

FUEL TANKER

BAGGAGE TRAILER

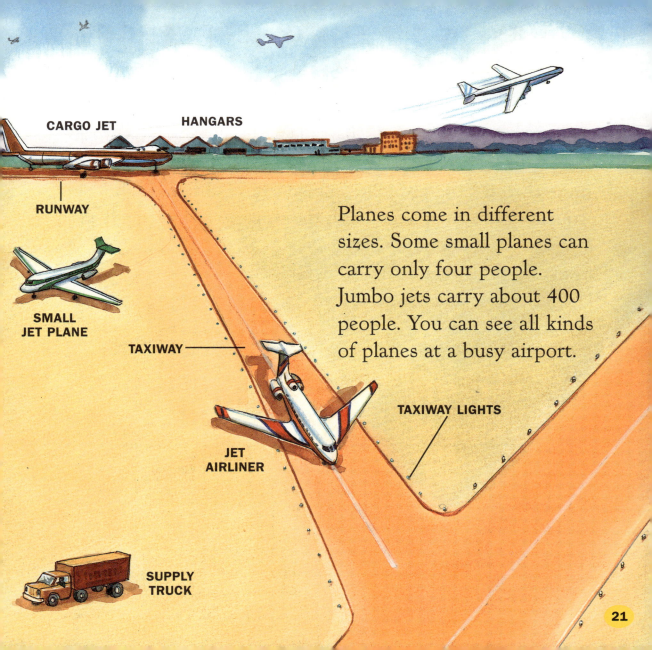

CARGO JET

HANGARS

RUNWAY

SMALL
JET PLANE

TAXIWAY

JET
AIRLINER

TAXIWAY LIGHTS

SUPPLY
TRUCK

Planes come in different sizes. Some small planes can carry only four people. Jumbo jets carry about 400 people. You can see all kinds of planes at a busy airport.

WHY DON'T SOME AIRPLANES HAVE PROPELLERS?

Jet planes don't need propellers. They have jet engines instead. The propeller moves a plane forward. When the pilot pushes in the throttle, the propeller spins faster and faster. The propeller pulls the plane down the runway and through the air.

Planes without propellers have special engines that burn jet fuel. The jet engines make the planes go.

TURBOPROP PLANE

JET PLANE

Think about what happens when you blow up a balloon and don't tie a knot in it. If you let the balloon go, the air rushes out. The balloon flies around the room.

A jet engine works a little like that. Fast-moving air or gases rush out the back of the jet engine and push the plane forward. A jet engine keeps taking in air so it can keep pushing air out.

HOW DOES A HELICOPTER FLY?

A helicopter's long rotor blades pull the helicopter straight up into the air—the same way an airplane's propeller pulls it down the runway. Short rotor blades on the helicopter's tail help keep the tail steady.

Helicopters aren't as fast as airplanes. But they can do things that airplanes can't do. Helicopters can hover, and they can take off and land without a runway.

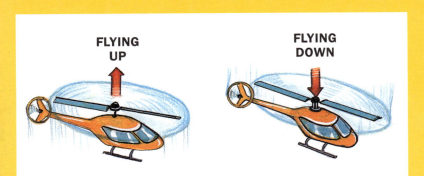

FLYING UP

FLYING DOWN

To fly a helicopter up or down, the pilot moves a control that tilts the rotor blades.

To fly forward, backward, or sideways for a turn, the pilot tilts the whole rotor in the direction he wants to go, as shown in the picture above.

HOW HiGH CAN AiRPLANeS FLY?

Planes fly high to stay above the clouds that bring bad weather. Large passenger jets usually fly 5 to 8 miles high (8 to 13 kilometers high). The Concorde is the highest-flying passenger plane. It zooms along 10 miles (16 kilometers) above the ground. That's twice as high as the highest mountain in the world.

High in the sky it's very cold. The air is so thin that people have trouble breathing. Flying high was uncomfortable for airplane passengers years ago. Now planes have special equipment to keep the air inside the cabin warm and breathable.

HOW DOES A PILOT KNOW WHERE THE PLANE IS GOING?

Before a plane takes off, the pilot studies a map called a flight chart. The flight chart shows highways, cities, and airports the plane will be passing over. The pilot stays on course by looking for these landmarks on the ground.

But pilots can't always see the ground. Sometimes planes fly high above the clouds. Sometimes it's dark and stormy outside. Then pilots depend on the compass, the clock, the computer, and the radio navigation equipment.

HOW FAST DO AIRPLANES GO?

Small planes with propellers fly about 175 miles per hour (280 kilometers per hour). That's more than twice as fast as a car on the highway.

Big passenger jets fly even faster—about 600 miles per hour (960 kilometers per hour).

The Concorde can fly 1,500 miles per hour (2,400 kilometers per hour). After it takes off it makes a huge booming sound, called a sonic boom.

The SR-71A military plane is one of the fastest planes in the world. It speeds across the sky at 2,000 miles per hour (3,200 kilometers per hour).

Test planes with rocket engines are even faster. Rocket planes can fly 4,500 miles per hour (7,200 kilometers per hour)!

Small propeller plane 175 mph (280 kph)

Jumbo jet 600 mph (960 kph)

Concorde 1,500 mph (2,400 kph)

SR-71A 2,000 mph (3,200 kph)

WHAT IS THE BIGGEST PLANE?

The biggest passenger plane is the Boeing 747-400. It carries more than 400 people and enough fuel to fly for about fifteen hours.

The C-5A Galaxy is an enormous military plane. It can carry a huge missile, two tanks, or 345 soldiers and their gear.

C-5A GALAXY

As you know by now, propeller or jet engines, specially shaped wings, and the moving parts on the wings and tail make an airplane fly.

The space shuttle has wings and a tail, but not an airplane engine. It can't take off and fly through the air. Huge rockets shoot the shuttle into space. When it lands, the shuttle soars to the ground like a glider.

The space shuttle is really a combination spaceship and glider, not an airplane.

SPACE SHUTTLE

Be a Junior Scientist!

You can be a junior scientist in your very own home. Turn your room into an airplane hangar. Assemble the two airplanes and observe the wonders of flight. Who knows? Maybe you will fly your own plane someday!

ASSEMBLY INSTRUCTIONS

The following assembly instructions should be followed for each plane model. Be careful to match each wing and stabilizer with each fuselage; they have matching letters. For instance, the letter A appears on all three pieces of plane A.

1.   Carefully insert the large wing in the slot at the front of the fuselage. The arrow on the wing should point toward the front of the plane. Continue sliding the wing until the notches line up at the center of the fuselage, making sure that the letter on the wing corresponds to the letter on the fuselage.

2.   Insert the small stabilizer in the back slot of the fuselage. The arrow on the stabilizer should point toward the front of the plane. Continue sliding the stabilizer into the slot until both sides of the stabilizer are the

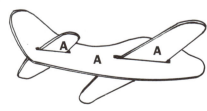

same length on either side of the fuselage, once again making sure that the letters on the stabilizer and fuselage match.

3. Clip the clear plastic tip to the nose section of the fuselage. (This will allow for more weight at the nose section for a longer, more stable flight.)

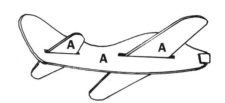

4. Grip the fuselage under the large wing and toss it forward in one smooth motion.

EXPERIMENTS, TEST FLIGHTS, AND PLANE GAMES

Your two airplanes are perfect for flying indoors in your bedroom or play area. A real pilot gives a new plane a flight test to see how it flies. You can give both of your planes several flight tests to find out what the planes will do.

Practice flying them until you can make your planes go where you want them to go. Experiment a little! Can you fly two planes at once?

Take your planes outside on a day when there's no wind. Which plane flies higher? Stand on your porch or deck and launch your planes. Which one stays in the air longer? Keep a chart showing your planes' flight records.

	Plane A	Plane B
Fastest flight		
Farthest flight		
Longest flight		
Highest flight		
Lowest flight		

Here are some plane games you can play with a friend:

Game 1.   First, give a plane to each player. Then set up small figures
around the room. Use plastic dinosaurs, soldiers, or cardboard
characters. See who can knock down the most by flying their
plane into the figures.

Game 2.   Set up an obstacle course for your planes inside or outside.
Fly your favorite plane through a hole cut in a section of
cardboard. Then fly it between two books. Fly it under a chair
and over the bed. Fly it through a tunnel made of cardboard.
How many throws did it take to get your plane through the
obstacle course? Can you go through the course in fewer
flights the second time?

CAN YOU ANSWER THESE QUESTIONS?

Which plane flies fastest? (pgs. 23, 26)

Which picture shows the yoke? (pg. 12)

Which plane was built first? (pg. 7)

Can you find these parts of a plane? (pgs. 10-11)

WING
TAILLIGHT
NOSE
FUSELAGE

Match the planes with their names. (pg. 26)

JUMBO JET
CONCORDE
PROPELLER PLANE